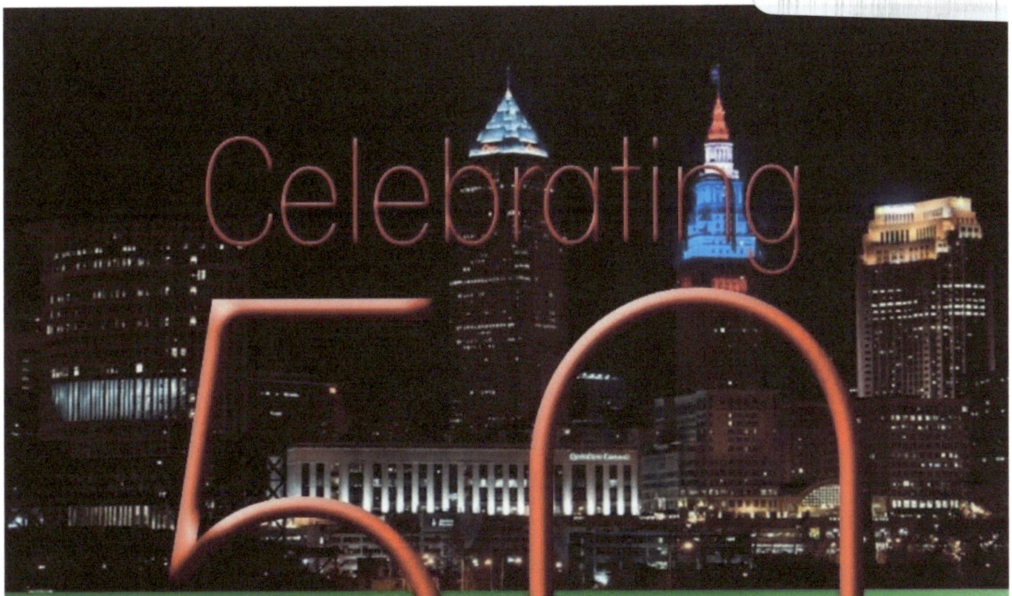

# Celebrating 50

## The Legacy of the Muntu Poets of Cleveland

Muntu Poets

Legacy

1968
2018

**Celebrating 50 - The Legacy of the Muntu Poets of Cleveland** © 2018 by K Kelly McElroy ; Russell Atkins ; with Muntu Poets : M.A Shaheed, Yaseen Assami, Robert Fleming, Art Nixon ; along with Vince Robinson; B Real; Danielle; and VitaGold.

All rights reserved. Printed in the United States of America. No part of this book may be used or reproduced in any manner whatsoever without written permission except in the case of brief quotations embodied in critical articles or reviews.

This book is a work of partial non-fiction. However, names, characters, businesses, organizations, places, events and incidents either are the product of the author's imagination or are used fictitiously. Any resemblance to actual persons, living or dead, events, or locales is entirely coincidental.

For information contact: info@uptownmediaventures.com

Book and Cover design by Team Uptown

ISBN: 978-1-68121-080-3
First Edition: February 2018

10 9 8 7 6 5 4 3 2

# Muntu Dedication

Dedicated to all the writers, poets, musicians, teachers, supporters, patrons, collaborators, and the all-around-cool-cats who feed the cultural tributary that is Black Life!

The Legacy Continues!

# The Original Muntu Poets

Russell Atkins
Norman Jordan

Sababa Akil

Hzal Anubewei  (Anthony Fudge)

Yaseen A Assami (Perry W Davis)

Sakki Beyti

Elmer Buford

Robert Fleming

Betty Flonney

Marty Friedman

Art Nixon

Amir Rashid

Bill Russell

Yahya A Sabur (John Hall)

Mutawaf A Shaheed (C E Shy)

**Russell Atkins**

# HERE IN THE

**CLEVELAND STATE UNIVERSITY
POETRY CENTER**

# Table of Contents

Foreword by Vince Robinson — 11

Introduction — 13

The Founding Fathers — 15
    Russell Atkins — 15
    Norman Jordan — 17
    The Legacy — 19

Recognition Long Overdue — 21

The Original Muntu Poets — 27
    Robert Fleming — 31
    M.A. Shaheed — 34
    Art Nixon — 38
    Yaseen Assami — 40
    Vince Robinson — 41

The Legacies — 45
    B Real — 45
    Danielle Dixon — 47

Celebrating 50 • 1968 - 2018
The Legacy of the Muntu Poets of Cleveland

| | |
|---|---|
| **VitaGold** | **48** |
| **The Poetic Gallery** | **49** |
| Russell Atkins | 49 |
|    DAWN (Rest Home) | 49 |
|    Evening Reflections In a Birdbath | 51 |
|    Flu As A Old War Movie | 53 |
| Norman Jordan | 55 |
|    Kuumba | 55 |
|    I Have Seen Them | 55 |
|    Popsicle Cold | 56 |
| Robert Fleming | 57 |
|    H E R O D | 57 |
|    J U J U | 58 |
|    Poems for Beginners | 59 |
| M.A. Shaheed | 63 |
|    Advancing | 63 |
|    Tabulations | 64 |
|    The Asterisk | 65 |

| | |
|---|---|
| **Art Nixon** | **67** |
| Highway Markers. | |
|     Review Mirrors | 67 |
| [ In Confidence] | 70 |
| Smooth Science | 72 |
| | |
| **Yaseen Assami** | **75** |
| A Glass of Lemonade | 75 |
| Gorilla Glue DUCT Tape | |
|     and Spit | 77 |
| Microwave Grits | 79 |
| | |
| **Vince Robinson** | **81** |
| STAND | 81 |
| | |
| **B Real** | **83** |
| America, Girl You Slippin' | 83 |
| Gil I Wanna Vibe | 87 |
| | |
| **Danielle Dixon** | **89** |
| Ain't Dat Some Shit | 89 |
| Beware | 92 |
| I Am Fabulous | 93 |

| | |
|---|---|
| **VitaGold** | **95** |
|    I Am The Reason | 95 |
|    Iron Sharpens Iron | 96 |
| | |
| **K Kelly** | **97** |
|    I Know… | 97 |
|    Star Child | 100 |
|    True Love | 102 |
| | |
| **About the Author** | **105** |

# Foreword

There's something about the DNA of a city that breeds creativity. Something about the collective experience of a people wedded by circumstances and history motivates some of us to use words to capture the nuances of our lives and share them in such a way that others, namely, the world becomes aware and informed.

Cleveland is one of those cities. Historically, Langston Hughes made an indelible mark on the cultural landscape with his poetry and writings, speaking to the ills of society while shedding insight on the value of Black pride and self-worth.

As he did, his impact was felt in communities across the nation grappling with a never-ending quest for civil and human rights. Then came the 60's, replete with uprisings fueled by unrest over the blatant disregard for Black life demonstrated by overt brutality and covert subversion.

It is out of that backdrop of urban reality that the voice of the Muntu Poets was born. It is a voice bathed in fire of El Hajj Malik Shabazz, Kwame Toure', Nikki Giovanni and Amiri Baraka, on a bed of Coltrane, Shepp and Mingus. It is the pedagogy of an African-centered curriculum parceled out in bite-sized morsels of music and verbs of different flavors. From Russell Atkins to Mutawaf Shaheed, Norman Jordan to Art Nixon and the countless others in this stew, the diversity of voices pick up where Langston trod, but in their own unique and contrasting recipes.

Then enter the new voices, B Real, Danielle Dixon, VitaGold, and Kelly McElroy, perhaps a newer iteration, nouveau Muntu, if you will. The work seems reflective of a slightly different introspection at times, while capturing the pulse of socially connected/disconnected reality of the day. The struggle continues over the underpinnings of hope and a yearning for change.

The journey unfolds in this roadmap provided by the eyes and ears of a nation: the Muntu Poets.

Vince Robinson
December 2017

# Introduction

A legacy is defined as a bequest, a gift, an inheritance - something that is acquired without compensation. Inspiration can be defined as an arousal of the mind to special unusual activity or creativity. The Muntu Poets have certainly fit these definitions as a socially and culturally significant force in the Black Community, as well as the community-at-large.

Over the years and entering into the new millennium, the renown of the master poet Russell Atkins seemed to wane with the changing times.

Eventually, Norman Jordan, Atkins' co-creator of the Muntu Poets poetry workshop, who gained notoriety as a poet laureate and went on to achieve international recognition, transitioned to the next life. However, Jordan left an indelible legacy.

The reason 1968 was chosen as a pivotal year, and not 1966 (the year the group was formed), for the Muntu Poets is because the group last met the day before the Glenville Riots in Cleveland, Ohio. This type of event was predicted by the poets. The climate in the community reached a boiling point by then! The semi-formal sessions that began in late 1966 were now a thing of the past.

A dormancy ensured as the young poets grew up, obtained employment, and raised young families. However, that Muntu seed really was just sprouting. That seed eventually bore much fruit. Some of the Muntu Poet workshop members, like Robert Fleming (who now resides in New York City), gained wide recognition in the literary and journalism world.

M.A. Shaheed, Art Nixon, Yaseen Assami, Robert Fleming, along with others helped propel the growth of a Cleveland based independent publishing house named Uptown Media Joint Ventures. Members of the Original Muntu Poets banded together to publish an anthology in recognition of Russell Atkins, *The Muntu Poets Anthology Volume 2, 47 Years Later with Russell Atkins.* Uptown Publishing has over 80 titles, of which many are derived from the Muntu Poets or the "Legacies."

Shaheed spearheaded the formation of the Legacies, which is a collaboration of various younger poets who have come together in recognition of the seed that was planted by the Muntu Poets. Due to the efforts of Shaheed and others, several albums have been released in 2017 and many more are in production.

The fact that pioneers and trailblazers such as Russell Atkins and Norman Jordan took the time to reach out to others, especially young people in the community, is priceless.

The story of this inspirational legacy is the theme of this book. I have personally witnessed and benefited tremendously from this legacy. I plan on doing my part to continue the legacy by supporting and feeding the cultural tributary that is Black Life!

K Kelly McElroy
Cleveland, Ohio
October 26, 2017

# The Founding Fathers

## Russell Atkins

As stated by writer Kevin Prufer, in his work, *Russell Atkins: On the life and work of an American master:*

> "His plays *The Abortionist* and *The Corpse* debuted in 1954. Following this, he founded *Free Lance, A Magazine of Poetry and Prose* in 1950 with his friend, Adelaide Simon, with the first issue containing an introduction by Langston Hughes.[3] It attracted writers from all over the world, leading the now-defunct *Black World* to call it "the only Black literary magazine of national importance in existence."[2] In 1959 Free Lance Press began publishing books, with a volume of poetry from Conrad Kent Rivers.[3] *Free Lance* was under Atkins leadership for more than

two decades, and allowed Atkins to correspond with writers from across the country."

Atkins was one of the first concrete poets in the United States. Concrete poetry is a term for visual or shape poetry, in which the words on the page are arranged in such a way as to enhance a poem's meaning. He was also an innovator in poetic drama. Much of Atkins' most challenging work—including the verse drama *The Abortionist,* was published in *Free Lance*.

The famed Langston Hughes, was a friend of Russell Atkins, and Hughes introduced Atkins' work to magazines. Hughes read his poems at the University of Michigan and the University of Chicago. Notably, Marrianne Moore read Atkin's work on the radio in 1951. Carl Van Vechten was a prominent adherent of Atkins' work, as well.

By the epoch of the 1960s Russell Atkins had become a significant literary figure in Cleveland and a fixture in the Northeast Ohio literary and musical scene. Atkins, a major poet-editor-composer, used revolutionary musical structures in his writing, co-founded possibly the oldest black-owned literary magazine, *Free Lance*, in 1950. The Free Lance was a Magazine of Poetry and Prose Atkins' founded with friend, Adelaide Simon. The first issue contained an introduction by Langston Hughes, and Free Lance continued under Atkins' leadership for more than two decades.

Atkins' books included several notable works as: P*henomena* (1961), *Objects* (1963), *Heretofore* (1968), *Maleficum* (1971), *Objects 2* (1973), and *Here in The* (1976).

It could reasonably said that Atkins dwelt in a well-deserved academic and literary ivory tower, yet his cautious belief that poetry was essential to Black culture compelled him to reach out into the inner city urban community and plant seeds there, as well.

# Norman Jordan

On the other side of the fence was Norman Jordan. Jordan was educated and learned just as Atkins, who ultimately earned a Bachelor's degree from West Virginia University in theater and a Master's degree in African American studies from Ohio State University. However, Jordan knew the "pulse" of the streets. Akins was somewhat removed from that scene.

As written by Robert Fleming, in the foreword for the book, *The Muntu Poets Anthology, 47 Years Later with Russell Atkins*, "Born in West Virginia and relocating to Cleveland, Norman Jordan was an internationally known poet and playwright. His work has appeared in more than 40 poetry collections, making him one of the most popular voices in the Black Arts Movement. He wrote five books of poetry, including *Destination Ashes, Above Maya, Where Do People In Dreams Come From and Other Poems, Two Books,* and *Sing Me Different*. Ever seeking knowledge, Jordan returned to his hometown, Ansted, in 1977, earning a Bachelor's degree from West Virginia University in theater and a Master's degree in African American studies from Ohio State University. He died in 2015, with many in the literary world mourning his loss."

Celebrating 50 • 1968 - 2018
The Legacy of the Muntu Poets of Cleveland

As a poet and a playwright, Norman Jordan's poems have appeared in many anthologies including: The Poetry of the Negro, Black Fire, Make a Joyful Sound: Poems for Children by A.A. Poets, In Search of Color Everywhere: A Collection of A.A. Poetry, and Wild Sweet Notes: Fifty years of West Virginia Poetry 1950-1999. A voice and leading force in the Black Arts Movement, Jordan's work also appeared in journals dedicated to the movement such as Journal of Black Poetry and Black World. Jordan had also written two books of poetry: Destination: Ashes (1967) and Above Maya (1971).

Jordan was inducted into an exclusive group of poets named the Affrilachian Poets, in 2008. Jordan was also a collaborator, editor, a storyteller, and had taught at West Virginia University, among other schools.

Jordan was a key person in the formation of the Black Arts Movement. Jordan was a leading force in the Cleveland, Ohio Poetry Movement, and he worked closely with the Karamu House, the oldest African American theater in the United States, which served as a spring board for many African American artists, including Ruby Dee, Langston Hughes, along with many others. Cleveland became a notable point of circulation of ideas during the Black Arts Movement.

Jordan was very active in the community, especially with youth, serving as a director of Camp Washington-Carver for Culture and History for many years.

Jordan was the president and founder of the African American Arts and Heritage Academy (AAAHA), as well as the founder and director of the African American Heritage Family Tree Museum in Ansted.

# The Legacy

As contemporaries, Atkins and Jordan both were deeply involved in the literary, theatrical, and music scenes. Atkins' and Jordan's visions coalesced during the tumult and civil unrest of the mid to late 1960s. Atkins was somewhat removed from the "streets," as it were. He sought to reach out to young Blacks who were not necessarily exposed to the more mainstream literary and arts community, as he was. Jordan was a key in implementing this vision.

As a result of their shared vision, the Muntu Poets poetry workshop came into existence in the late 1960s to bring literary expression to the "hood." Atkins was somewhat hesitant to start this workshop with a group of sometimes incorrigible young inner city youth. But the challenging times spurred both Atkins and Jordan forward.

It was a time as described by Robert Fleming, an original Muntu Poet from Cleveland, a noted New York writer, and a protégé of Russell Atkins in the book, *The Muntu Poets Anthology, 47 Years Later with Russell Atkins*:

> "It was a time of protest, action, and honoring the choice to walk upright and proud. It was a time of Malcolm X, Amiri Baraka, Sonia Sanchez, Nikki Giovanni, the Umbra Poets, the Negritude Poets - Cesaire, Damas, Diop, and Senghor, the Lotus Press in Detroit, Broadside Press and the Third World Press in Chicago. It was the hard-charging juju of the New Music, with high priests such as Coltrane, Albert Ayler, Archie Shepp, Sonny Rollins, Marion Brown, Sun Ra and Cecil Taylor. And the pistol-packing Black Panthers. Spark, rhythm, consciousness."

# Celebrating 50 • 1968 - 2018
## The Legacy of the Muntu Poets of Cleveland

Original Muntu Poets (left to right): Mutawaf Shaheed, Sababa Akili, Norman Jordan, and Bill Russell after a poetry reading for the Cleveland Ethical Society

The last Muntu meeting occurred on July 23, 1968, the same date of the shoot-outs and upheaval that commenced the Glenville Riots. However, under Atkins' and Jordan's leadership, the workshop had successfully planted the literary seed which certainly positively influenced all of the workshop attendees.

Nevertheless, the literary seed had been planted. Who knew when that seed might sprout?...

# Recognition Long Overdue

The rebirth of the Muntu Poets and the ensuing Legacies began with the revitalization of M.A. Shaheed. Shaheed, like many of the original Muntu Poets, had the growing responsibilities of raising a family. His becoming a religious leader, also, impeded the frequency of his literary expression. A glacial period set in for a number of years…

However, that poetic literary seed that was planted by the Muntu Poets of Cleveland poetry workshop eventually sprouted through the cracks in the concrete. He had been published in two anthologies and in the 60's in the Muntu Poets book of poems done by Russell Atkins and Norman Jordan.

He started back writing again in late 1990's; when he started writing novellas and flash fiction, in addition to poetry. He joined the Cyril D. Dostal poetry workshop in Lyndhurst, Ohio at the Cuyahoga County library in 2011 to hone his writing skills.

Since that time, Shaheed's creative output has been extraordinary indeed! At the time of the publishing of this book Shaheed has published over 40 books under his pen name "C.E. Shy." In addition to that he has participated in over a dozen anthologies.

"I give eternal credit to my mentor Russell Atkins, along with Norman Jordan and other master poets, who planted that seed in me. Life circumstances may have side-tracked me, yet the inspiration never went away," says Shaheed.

Not too long after Shaheed joined the Cyril D. Dostal poetry workshop in Lyndhurst, Ohio, the name of Russell Atkins began to circulate among the workshop members. By a fortuity, Atkins was found by key workshop members. Shaheed's and Atkin's relationship as study and mentor, respectively, resurrected into a thriving force.

# Celebrating 50 • 1968 - 2018
## The Legacy of the Muntu Poets of Cleveland

By the time 2014 approached, many events that were intended to give Russell Atkins his "just due" developed in throws.

In October, 2014 members of the, recently named, Cyril A. Dostal poetry workshop held an event at the East Cleveland Public Library wherein Russell Atkins was re-awarded an honorary doctoral degree from Cleveland State University. Tragically, many of Atkins' works were destroyed when he was hospitalized.

In the same month of October, 2014, as an original Muntu Poet, Shaheed spearheaded the development of a local Cleveland-based indie publishing house named Uptown Media Joint Ventures, which led to the publication of many works by many authors over the next three years up to the publication of this book.

(Russell Atkins (seated) with Charles Pinkney (middle) and Nathan Oliver)

In January 2016, The *Muntu Poets of Cleveland* book of poetry that was originally published by Russell Atkin's Free Lance Poets Press in 1968, was republished by Uptown Media Joint Ventures.

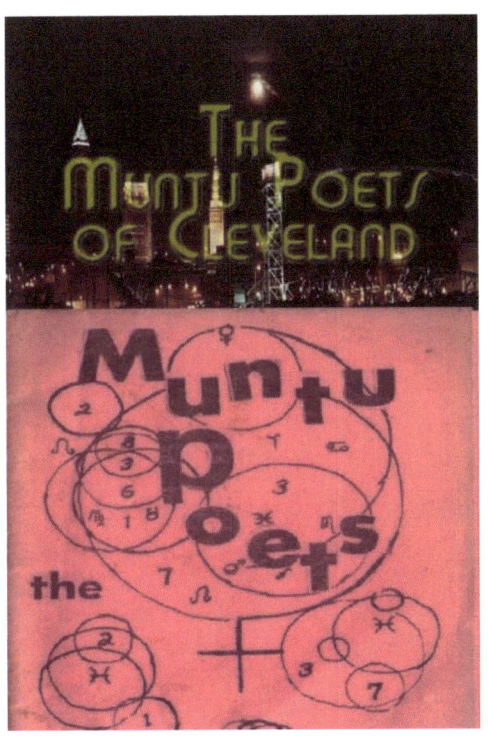 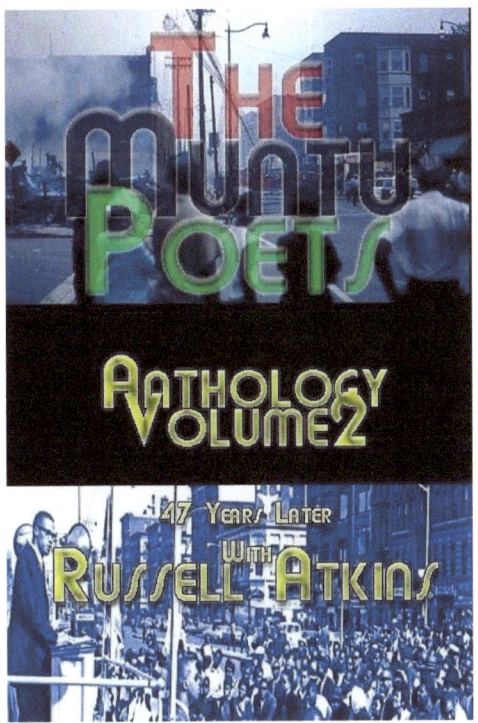

That same month, a second anthology was published by Uptown: *The Muntu Poets Anthology, 47 Years Later with Russell Atkins,* after various Muntu Poets from across the country came together to make that publication happen.

In November, 2016, The Cyril D. Dostal Poetry Workshop held an event in recognition of Russell Atkins. That event celebrated the publication of the anthology, *In The Company of Russell Atkins*. The event featured many scholars and poets who traveled from other states to speak and pay homage to Atkins.

That same month a film short entitled, *Muntu Poets*, was presented at the Orlando Urban Film Festival. The film highlighted the

# Celebrating 50 • 1968 - 2018
## The Legacy of the Muntu Poets of Cleveland

renewed vigor and endeavors of the Muntu Poets and their supporters, which was reflected by album releases, poetry events, and the triumph of the publication of *The Muntu Poets Anthology, 47 Years Later with Russell Atkins*.

In February 2017, Russell Atkins was given senior recognition by TV20 Cleveland as a literary luminary in the world of poetry. Atkins' readings of "Night and a Distant Church," "Train Yard at Night," and "It's Here In The" were filmed by the television station.

In February, 2017 Muntu Poets from various parts of the United States gathered to perform for their first show after a hiatus of many years. The show was held at the Greg L. Reese Performing Arts Center at the East Cleveland Public Library. The show was a success and the Poets used varied mediums such as music and videos in their performance.

Original Muntu Poets after performance at the East Cleveland Public Library
(l to r) M.A. Shaheed, Yahya Abdussabur, Yaseen Assami, and Sababa Akili

In May, 2017 Atkins was awarded the very prestigious Cleveland Arts Prize for Lifetime Achievement, along with a $10,000 award. The award was presented at the Museum of Contemporary Art, Cleveland (MOCA).

Russell Atkins (seated) along with other Cleveland Arts Prize recipients

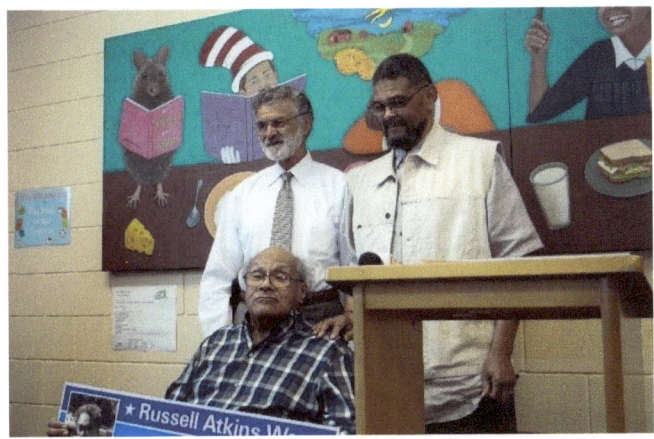

Lastly, but certainly not least, in June, 2017 a portion of Grand Avenue in Cleveland, Ohio was renamed: "Russell Atkins Way, Grand Avenue." Atkins was given a replica of the new street sign by Mayor Frank Jackson. The event was well attended and was catered by Uptown Media Joint Ventures.

"All-in-all it's wonderful to see Russell finally getting his just due, at the ripe young age of 92," stated M.A. Shaheed, a major player in fomenting this long overdue recognition.

# Celebrating 50 • 1968 - 2018
## The Legacy of the Muntu Poets of Cleveland

M.A. Shaheed, Russell Atkins, with filmmaker Khalil Pedizi

Russell Atkins with Uptown Media Joint Ventures publisher, K Kelly McElroy

# The Original Muntu Poets

As contemporaries, Atkins and Jordan both were deeply involved in the literary, theatrical, and music scenes. Atkins' and Jordan's visions coalesced during the tumult and civil unrest of the mid to late 1960s. Atkins was somewhat removed from the "streets," as it were. He sought to reach out to young Blacks who were not necessarily exposed to the more mainstream literary and arts community, as he was. Jordan was a key in implementing this vision.

As a result of their shared vision, the Muntu Poets poetry workshop came into existence in the late 1960s to bring literary expression to the "hood." Atkins was somewhat hesitant to start this workshop with a group of sometimes incorrigible young inner city youth. But the challenging times spurred both Atkins and Jordan forward.

A host of other young people in the Muntu Poet workshop were positively influenced even if Atkins may had been wondering about many of these, sometime militant, young attendees.

One of the first concrete expressions of the workshop was the publication: *The Muntu Poets of Cleveland*, which was first published by Atkins in 1968 under the FREE LANCE POETS PRESS. Atkins gave each young writer a voice to convey their thoughts. As of 2017, this very book is being used in a local college course.

The last Muntu meeting occurred on July 23, 1968, the same date of the shoot-outs and upheaval that commenced the Glenville Riots. However, under Atkins' and Jordan's leadership, the workshop had successfully planted the literary seed which certainly positively influenced all of the workshop attendees.

# Celebrating 50 • 1968 - 2018
## The Legacy of the Muntu Poets of Cleveland

Mutawaf (M.A.) Shaheed, a poet who found purpose with the group and author of over 40 books, exclaimed: "The (Muntu Poet's) voices of dissent were the loudest and it was this group that raised their voices everywhere they went. They were the only group of poets in the city doing that. They felt that everyone else was putting honey and perfume on shit."

"I do believe that we were called together to do a very important and great thing by some unknown force or forces in our lives," recalls Yaseen A. Assami, a Muntu member and published author. "Us being in Muntu was a part of that calling. There were no other group of any kind, just us and our dreams STRAIGHT NO CHASER."

Yaseen Assami

A dormancy occurred when many of these young Muntu Poets grew up, found professions (or jobs), and had families to provide for. However, that seed was still there and many of the original Muntu Poets like Sababa Akili, Hzal Anubewei (Anthony Fudge), Yaseen A. Assami (Perry W. Davis), Sakki Beyti, Elmer Buford, Robert Fleming, Betty Flannoy, Marty Freeman, Omarr Majied, Art Nixon, Amir Rashidd, Bill Russell, Yahya A. Sabur (Jon Hall), and Mutawaf A. Shaheed (C. E. Shy) still became published authors and accomplished in their respective fields of endeavors.

Over the years and entering into the new millennium, Atkins' renown seemed to wane with the changing times. However, that Muntu seed really was just sprouting. Some of the workshop members like Robert Fleming, who now resides in New York City, gained wide recognition in the literary and journalism fields.

M.A. Shaheed eventually reignited his literary efforts in the new millennium with his membership in the Cyril L. Dostal Poetry Workshop held at the Lyndhurst branch of the Cuyahoga County Library presided by writer, Robert McDonough.

B Real and M.A. Shaheed Performing at Larchmere Arts, Cleveland, Ohio

M.A. Shaheed, Art Nixon, Yaseen Assami, Robert Fleming, along with others helped propel the growth of a Cleveland based independent publishing house named Uptown Media Joint Ventures. Members of the Original Muntu Poets banded together to publish an anthology in recognition of Russell Atkins, *The Muntu Poets Anthology, 47 Years*

# Celebrating 50 • 1968 - 2018
## The Legacy of the Muntu Poets of Cleveland

*Later with Russell Atkins.* Uptown Publishing has over 50 titles which are derived from Muntu Poets.

A group of Original Muntu Poets (including Elmer Buford, Yahya Abdussabur, Art Nixon, M.A. Shaheed, and Yaseen Assami) released two musical spoken word albums in 2017 entitled: *Straight Up!* and *Ain't No Change!* Many of the poets have released albums of their own.

Key members of the Muntu Poets include Robert Fleming, M.A. Shaheed, Art Nixon, and Yaseen Assami. Due to the stellar efforts of these key members, the legacy of the Muntu Poets certainly continues…

# Robert Fleming

Robert Fleming certainly is an extraordinary example of how inspiration can pay off in huge dividends. Fleming was an original Muntu Poet as a teen and soaked up the essence and vibe of that poetry workshop that was led by Russell Atkins and Norman Jordan.

Fleming became a freelance journalist and editor, eventually, working as a writer-consultant with ex-CBS News president Fred Friendly, boss of the legendary Edward R. Morrow for the PBS TV show, Media and Society, after graduating from Columbia University's Journalism school.

Fleming served as a reporter for the *New York Daily News*, throughout the 1980s and into the 1990s, earning several honors including a New York Press Club award and a Revson Fellowship in 1990. He worked as a freelance editor and book doctor at Random House's imprint, One World. He taught courses in film and journalism at The New School. His articles and reviews have appeared in many publications such as *The New York Times, The Washington Post, U.S. News and World Report, Essence, Black Enterprise, Omni, Black Issues Book Review, Quarterly Black Review, and Publishers Weekly.*

# Celebrating 50 • 1968 - 2018
## The Legacy of the Muntu Poets of Cleveland

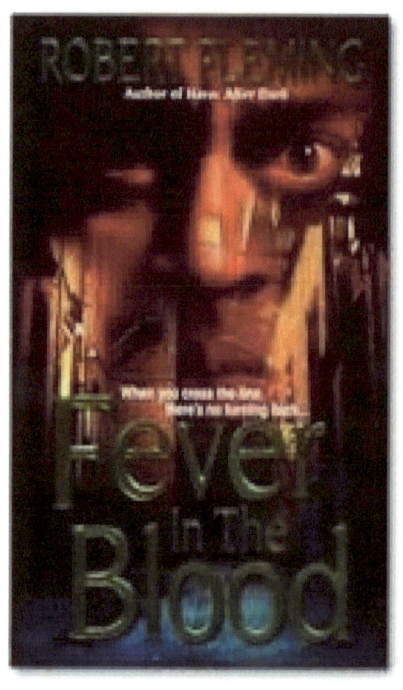

He has written several non-fiction books such as *Rescuing A Neighborhood, The Success of Caroline Jones Inc., The Wisdom of the Elders, and The African-American Writer's Handbook.* His fiction consists of such works as *Fever In The Blood, Havoc After Dark: Tales of Terror, Gift of Faith, Gift of Truth, and Gift of Revelation.* He edited three anthologies, *After Hours, Intimacy,* and *The Muntu Poets - 47 Years later with Russell Atkins.*

Flemings' contribution to the tributary of Black Culture remains unabated with the release of titles such as: *Free Jazz - Creative Originality, Controlled Surprise* (2016) and *Rasta, Babylon, Jamming - The Music and Culture of Roots Culture (2017).*

Fleming's success is inspiring and contagious. Fleming, along with other Muntu Poets like M.A. Shaheed, have certainly propelled the rebirth of a literary legacy, for which we all should be eternally grateful.

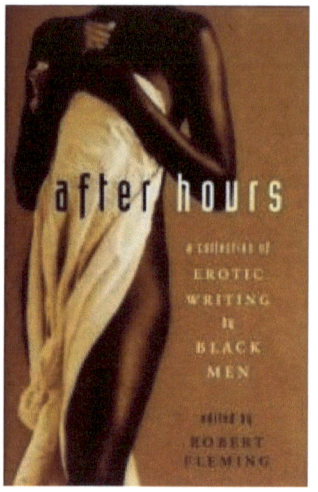

Celebrating 50 • 1968 - 2018
The Legacy of the Muntu Poets of Cleveland

# M.A. Shaheed (aka C.E. Shy)

Mutawaf A. Shaheed writes under the pen name of "C.E. Shy." He had been writing since the seventh grade. After graduating, he worked at the White Motors Company, where he was involved with the company's newspaper. He started a column called: "The Poets Corner," which was his first published work.

He moved to Sweden after he left the "States" with a one way ticket. He met an English photographer and wrote narratives for photographs that would be sold to newspapers and magazines in Europe.

After returning to the States, he joined a poetry workshop, the Muntu Poets, run by the noted master poet and musician Russell Atkins and Norman Jordan, who became an internationally renowned poet himself, from 1966 to 1968. Subsequently, Shaheed became a bassist with the famed Cleveland jazzman Albert Ayler.

He stopped writing for years, but later started back writing again in late 1990's, when he started writing novellas and flash fiction, in addition to poetry. He joined the longest running poetry workshop in Northeast Ohio, at the county library; located in Lyndhurst, Ohio; in 2011 to hone his writing skills. He has been published in several anthologies. His became a co-author in the 1960's with the publication of the *Muntu Poets of Cleveland* anthology of poems, under the tutelage of Russell Atkins and Norman Jordan.

During his hiatus Shaheed married and raised a family. After he recommenced his literary efforts in the 1990's, just like when Miles Davis returned from his sojourn to kick a narcotics habit, he made up for lost time in earnest! Shaheed's published output has been rather prolific considering that he published, in less than three years, over 40 books and counting. He published all those titles with the Cleveland, Ohio publishing house Uptown Media Joint Ventures (http://uptownmediaventures.com).

His literary works under his pen name C.E. Shy include: *Time Share, Substitions, Eclections 2 & 3, Powhims and Proz; The House, Stories - The Long and Short of It Vol. 1 & 2; Me and Maysun, Approaching the Ninth Deminsion; Raw forms, Structures and Vicissitudes of the Neighborhood; Deliver Me From Unconsciousness, The Visit, The Door at the End of the Hall, Point Blank! Eclections 4, The Glimpse - A Remote View, A Frayed, Mixed Feelings, Pens and Needles, Five Minutes Pass*

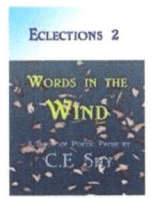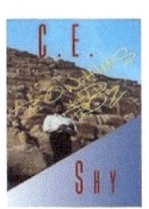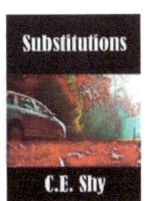
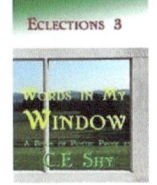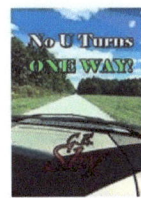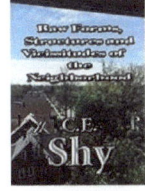

# Celebrating 50 • 1968 - 2018
## The Legacy of the Muntu Poets of Cleveland

*Midnight, Sketchings, PTSD - Poems That Say Dream, Traveling in the Light, Transparent S, Tuned In, More Questions Than Answers, Balance, If Only I Could, Zero at the End of the Rainbow, Miles To Go While I Weep, Signs and Signals, Watch Out, A Knock On The Door,* and *Chapter Z.*

Under Shaheed's oversight, the original *Muntu Poets of Cleveland* anthology of poems was republished in January, 2016. During that same month, the *Muntu Poets – Anthology Volume 2, 47 Years Later with Russell Akins* was published, as well. A remarkable journey that took all the Muntu Poets less than two months to complete from beginning to end.

Shaheed's expressions are not limited to the literary. The resurgence of the Muntu Poets is reflected by several albums of poetry with music that are set for release throughout the year in 2017. The poetry is accompanied by many styles of music including jazz, rap, classical, the blues, EDM, along with many other elements. Shaheed goes by the moniker "Mr. Gentleman," and has completed three albums: *Perspective Now is Then*, *Nomenclature (which was released in 2017)*, and *Point Blank!*

Shaheed has coproduced a documentary short film about the Muntu Poets, *The Muntu Poets Legacy*, which pays due homage to Russell Atkins and Norman Jordan. This film debuted at the Orlando Urban Film Festival on November 12, 2016.

Shaheed is an Imam of a local masjid and a member of a national Muslim (community) (Jaamat,) Called Al Ummah. From 1968 until 1973, he was the head of a very successful prison rehab program that was located in seven prisons in the State of Ohio.

Shaheed has lived in Egypt, Dubai, London, Paris, Stockholm, Sweden. I have spent time in Senegal, Tunisia, Nigeria Trinidad, Guyana, South America Saudi Arabia, Bahrain and Abu Dhabi, and the Artic Circle.

Shaheed's renown has grown by leaps and bounds as he has been invited to speak to various literary, poetry, and educational venues including the NIA Poetry Workshop of the Cleveland Public Library (MLK Branch); the 2016 Men's Adult Literary Discussion Forum of the Cleveland Public Library (Addison Branch); the SUNY (Oneonta) Departments of History and Africana and Latino Studies, Black History Month Discussion; along with many other entities.

M.A. Shaheed accompanied by many of his books

Celebrating 50 • 1968 - 2018
The Legacy of the Muntu Poets of Cleveland

# Art Nixon

Art Nixon became interested in writing after being introduced to poetry as a member of the Muntu Poets of Cleveland writing workshop headed by Russell Atkins. Art wrote and performed his poetry as a member of the Muntu Poets before going onto perform his poetry with various poetry groups around Cleveland and colleges around the state and on the local radio. His interest in writing led him to write essays and poetry for *Black Ascensions* literary and was one of four founders/editors which included Anthony fudge, Larry Howard, and Larry Wade [RIP] in the early 70s. The magazine was a first for Cuyahoga Community College and went on to earn honorable mention for college magazines in *Essence Magazine.*

A Cum Laude Graduate of Case Western Reserve University while married with a 3 year old son, who he brought to class frequently when babysitters weren't available. He's now a professor at a major Los Angeles University with two award winning books and a 3rd just released, *Race On The QT: Blackness in The Films of Quentin Tarantino*, University of Texas Press. Art published papers in Academic Journals as an undergraduate, while employed as a module tutor/instructor at Cuyahoga Community College's writing Lab. He was also employed as a visiting Poet-At-Large for the Cleveland Area Arts Council, introducing Greater Cleveland high school, middle school and elementary students to the first celebrated African American poets as early as 18th century slaves Phyllis Wheatly and Juniper Harmon, the Harlem Renaissance to contemporary urban poetry.

In Los Angeles, Art worked as a security guard for many years while writing screenplays, plays, and TV pilots, none of which he was able to get produced. He also wrote a weekly column for now defunct Las Vegas and Los Angeles black focused newspapers, Bronze News and Balance News for several years. Art has been published in several poetry anthologies, including *Black American Literature forum, The Drumming Between Us*, *Catch The Fire: A Cross-Generational Anthology of African American Poetry,* and others.

He is included in Columbia Granger's Index of African American Poets. Currently, Art is working on the novelization of one of his screenplays. It was published as a short story in Robert Fleming's Anthology of short stories, *Too Much Boogie: Erotic Remixed of The dirty Blues*. Art has two sons and two grandkids. He recently retired as front desk manager at the renown Beverly Hilton Hotel.

Nixon released a dynamic musical spoken word album in 2017 entitled: *Wishroot Meditations*, under the Uptown Records label. Also, in 2017, Nixon participated remotely in the Muntu Poets reunion show that was held at the Greg L. Reese Performing Arts Center at the East Cleveland Public Library. Nixon still actively writes and has publication of literary works pending.

# Yaseen Assami

Yaseen Assami was born Perry Wesley Davis in 1948 on November 12 in Knoxville, Tennessee. After high school he moved to Cleveland, Ohio.

After moving to Cleveland, he meet several of his long-time friends and Russell Atkins. He, subsequently, became a part of the Muntu Poets. His stay with the Muntu Poets was of short duration but his involvement was very influential and important part of his development as a youth and as a young expressionist writer.

Assami published a book of his poetic works entitled: *From Realism to Surrealism* in 2016. Assami also released a superb musical spoken word album in 2017 entitled: *Tymeless Voices*, under the Uptown Records label. Assami played a significant role in the Muntu Poets reunion show that was held at the Greg L. Reese Performing Arts Center at the East Cleveland Public Library in 2017.

Assami counts Atkins as a mentor and very dear friend; a person of unparalleled talent and creative ability. Mr. Assami counts his association with Russell Atkins as an honor. He also has valued relationships with other writers and poets who feel the same.

# Vince Robinson

Although he is not an original Muntu Poet, Vince Robinson certainly has proved to be an instrumental force in the rebirth of the Original Muntu Poets. Robinson's moniker as a cultural advocate has proved to be completely apropos and accurate.

Robinson graduated from Kent State University with a Bachelor of Arts Degree, cum laude. He currently co-hosts *360 Info Network*, airing on WERE-AM 1490 Radio in Cleveland and internationally on Black Planet Radio.com. He is also a director, producer, and host of the television program *Open Door* on Cable 9, Spectrum Cable in Summit County, Ohio.

He is the former host of JazzPoetry at the Cleveland Museum of Art, Robin's Nest and Another Level. He currently serves as host of the NeoSoulPoetry Open Mic Series, a spoken word cultural event held in Cleveland, Ohio. An accomplished slam poet, Vince was a member of the Cleveland Poetry Slam Teams that competed in the National Poetry Slam in Chicago (2003) and St. Louis (2004). He has been the featured poet at venues around the state of Ohio.

He is also an author. His first book, *Got Words?*, was published in April, 2015 by Parablist Publishing House, Inc.

Robinson is a public speaker and has appeared at several schools in Cleveland. In January 2001, he was the featured speaker at the Bradley

Center, in suburban Pittsburgh, Pennsylvania. He was also the Keynote Speaker for the Jubilee Day Program of the Ross County NAACP in 2016.

Most recently, he was the emcee of the Cleveland Urban League's Men of Distinction Award program (June 2013), which honored television news anchor Leon Bibb of WEWS TV 5, legendary Cleveland Glenville High School coach Ted Ginn Sr., and urologist Dr. Charles Modlin, among others, at John Carroll University.

He has been recognized by Cleveland City Council for promoting literacy and history, working closely with Cleveland City Councilman Kevin Conwell and his band, Vince Robinson & The Jazz Poets. Vince Robinson & The Jazz Poets have been performing in the Cleveland area and other locations in the Midwest since1997, including the Rock & Roll Hall of Fame and Museum, the Cleveland Museum of Art and others. The group was featured on WVIZ TV25's cultural arts program *Applause* on PBS.

He is a former news reporter for radio stations WERE-AM (Cleveland), WJMO-AM (Cleveland), WHLO-AM (Akron) and WKNT-AM (Kent), producing reports that aired nationally on CBS Radio news. His syndicated radio program *Reflections: A Moment in Music History* aired on stations throughout the state of Ohio with the Ohio Lottery serving as its sponsor.

In addition to radio, he produced and co-hosted *Down to Business*, a television show that aired on WOIO Channel 19 in Cleveland.

A member of the American Federation of Radio and Television Artists, he has been involved the production of documentaries and films and is a voice over announcer. He filmed his first documentary for Wilberforce University in Israel in 1992.

In addition to film projects, Vince is a photo-journalist with credits including Echelon Magazine, Crusader Arts and Entertainment News,

Phenomenal Woman Magazine and Cleveland's East Side Daily News. His specialty is jazz photography, with an extensive collection of photographs that include Miles Davis, Ella Fitzgerald, Nancy Wilson and many notable artists dating back to the early eighties.

His photography was also featured internationally on *Comedy from the Caribbean*, a comedy television series filmed in the Bahamas and Jamaica with host A.J. Jamal and guests that included comedians Steve Harvey and Drew Carey. African American Golf Digest published photographs and an article he wrote on a Panama City, Panama course in 2015.

In addition to his artistic endeavors, Vince is a retired insurance professional. His professional career includes 10 years as a claims representative and 17 years in Risk and Compliance as a reinspector/trainer. He served as co-chair of the Inclusion Advisory Council for State Farm's Mid-America Zone in 2007 and was actively involved in Diversity and Inclusion efforts within the organization.

Vince currently is the co-owner of Larchmere Arts, a combination photography studio, art gallery and performance venue. There he hosts a bi-weekly spoken word series called NeoSoul Poetry at Larchmere Arts. In August of 2016 and May 2017, he traveled to Ghana, West Africa to film a documentary for Kent State University. The film "The Real Africa" can be seen on YouTube. A collection of photographs from the film has been shown in the Uumbaji Gallery at Kent State University.

Celebrating 50 • 1968 - 2018
The Legacy of the Muntu Poets of Cleveland

Vince Robinson playing with band at Larchmere Arts

Some members of the Legacies - Channita, B Real and Danielle Dixon

# The Legacies

The Muntu Poets certainly are actively passing the baton to the next generation. Original Muntu Poet M.A. Shaheed certainly has been in the forefront of the passing of the baton. Shaheed has teamed up with next-generation artists like B Real and Danielle at local Cleveland shows. They performed at venues like Larchmere Arts and the East Cleveland Public Library.

Many of the Original Muntu Poets have been instrumental in the on-going success of the indie publishing company Uptown Media Joint Ventures. The most prominent advancers have been M.A. Shaheed, who has published over 40 books under the imprint, and Robert Fleming who has teamed up with publisher K Kelly McElroy to publish two culturally important books on jazz and reggae, respectively.

The Legacy has sprouted and takes multitudinous forms. Many projects are in the works like an anthology album for the benefit of Larchmere Arts entitled: *The Legacy Continues... A Muntu Poet Celebration of the Next Poetic Generation*. There are many, many talented spoken word artists and poets that have been influenced by the Muntu Poets, however, the following next generation poets have proven to be standout adherents of the Muntu poetic legacy.

## B Real

B-Real da poet/musician. Cleveland Born (McDonald House), paralyzed in 1996 in a car accident after being released from prison. He was going through a spiritual war and his prayers led him to poetry.

Celebrating 50 • 1968 - 2018
The Legacy of the Muntu Poets of Cleveland

Twenty years later with, as he puts it, "a clear thought (and peace of mind)," he shares his spiritual growth. The experience "of a man knocked down but not knocked out."

B-Real has performed all over Cleveland including City Hall and the Rock and Roll Hall of Fame. He has performed with the late great Amiri Baraka, he was taught the art of poetry and performed with David (Daveed) Nelson of the *Last Poets*. B-Real prides himself to be counted as one of the *Legacies*, under the tutelage of Cleveland's own *Muntu Poets*.

B Real released a musical spoken word album entitled: *Prayers for My People* in 2017 and continues to be a fixture in the spoken word scene in and around Northeast Ohio and adjoining states.

## Danielle Dixon

Danielle Dixon is a local poet and fiction writer from Cleveland Ohio. She got her Bachelor of Art from Kent State University. She has had her poetry published in the *Luna Negra* and *Inclusion Magazine*.

Danielle is an active alumna of the Cleveland School of the Arts where she assists with auditions each spring. Danielle has also been a feature NeoSoulPoet at Larchmere Arts and enjoys getting out to open mic events to test out new work.

Danielle is currently working on a collaboration project entitled: *The Legacy Continues... A Muntu Poet Celebration of the Next Poetic Generation*. and is looking to have a book published in the near future.

Danielle has a musical spoken word album entitled: *Sagittariusly BLUNT!* that was released in 2017.

Celebrating 50 • 1968 - 2018
The Legacy of the Muntu Poets of Cleveland

# VitaGold

Born in Cleveland, raised in New Jersey, VitaGold started writing poetry at the young age of 13. It was like a gift given to her to help her through the difficulties of puberty. Writing poetry for VitaGold was used to cover the pain and woes of life of a young teenager who was raised by her father. During this time, poetry became her passion, which helped sculpt her outlook on life. VitaGold returned back to her home town of Cleveland, Ohio to jump start her career.

In 2010, VitaGold joined the local spoken word scene performing in Cleveland and the surrounding areas. She has performed at several poetry venues like Dreamer's Bar; Grill Writer's Lounge; B Side Lounge; Urban Joe's Cafe - Soulful Expressions; The Stage - Purple Pages ;and Club 330 which is located in Akron, Ohio.

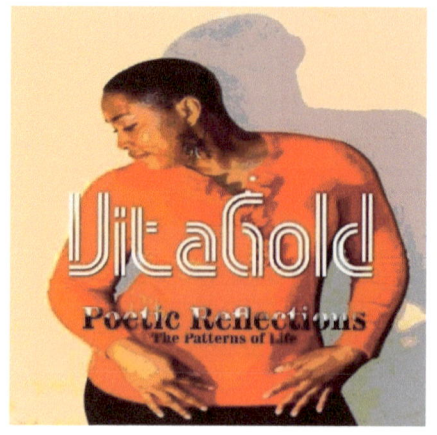

VitaGold released a musical spoken word album entitled: *Poetic Reflections* in 2017. VitaGold resides in California and continues to hone her craft.

# The Poetic Gallery

## Russell Atkins

## DAWN (Rest Home)

a hag'd like laughter
laughter that hags

now and then
down the hall
more laughed hag'd

thither of lit
is of a room thus'd to odd
with about shadow'd
     a door's nearby of at
     of/in, or/out, or/of, a door's from
COLD OPEN
    on somewhere

    aloud voices{ Next:
GOOD morning, good morning,}
    GOOD morning, sir,
GOOD morning all,
        (Good (Oh Really?
           Who says so?
beheld as day "dares" up to up'd

**Celebrating 50 • 1968 - 2018**
**The Legacy of the Muntu Poets of Cleveland**

    then falls
            to eve'd
meanwhile
then and now
hag'd laugh

K Kelly McElroy

# EVENING REELECTIONS IN A BIRDBATH

still    there in our birdbath
strangely eye like    light
repeated from the sky
ill of it there is the   so small
touch of a world's beware

some leafy shadows overs
from trees wind swell'd
the yard commonoplaces
now
        household sentiments,
            a rake, the lawnmower

until more stark than ever
in the round of the bowl
the always terror
stares out
        and out
        with a *lo!*

Celebrating 50 • 1968 - 2018
The Legacy of the Muntu Poets of Cleveland

K Kelly McElroy

# FLU AS A OLD WAR MOVIE

They're *the* strategists! They first clamp
Off the food supply from the port:
Heavy gunfire around the gut warehouse,
Like guards stabbed, one whipped cold
                  With a gun butt.

They seize the camouflaged brain radio
Scrambling the signals. Anyway, signals
Can't get through.   With flame throwers
They close in and in and tight.

While brain waves burn, a crack
Lung Team hits at breath.   They reconnoiter
Spraying the lobar regions - cold gook
From their Chemico-Warfare Division!

They've got one objective: the big
Muscle Center whose dynamos -
      huge pericardium masses – thunder
                  until whack,
      light is zapped, electricity's
out –
      *something* it out!

Celebrating 50 • 1968 - 2018
The Legacy of the Muntu Poets of Cleveland

# Norman Jordan

## Kuumba

Life is
Creative force
In motion
MOVE!!!

## I Have Seen Them

I have seen them trying
to sober up
to be heard
to listen
to live
Lord Knows, I have seen them.

I have seen them waiting
for relief
for a job
for winter to pass
for life
Yes Lord, I have seen them.

I have seen them crying
because it's too late
because they can't feed their babies
because they are tired of maybe
because they are afraid
Dear Lord yes, I have seen them
Praying
For miracles.

# Popsicle Cold

Now
that the story
has moved
out of the headlines
the widow
of the dead black hero
stands alone
at the public market
purchasing polluted pork
with government
food stamps

## Robert Fleming

# H  E  R  O  D

To listen them talk     I am

The monster     The slayer of newborns

The biblical murderer with the cold convict

face and frog voice     Why I never let

strangers sit too long in my house

or memories linger     Or the reason

for my orphan life

I never killed Christ     If they would

just listen    and forget the name

that I am.

# J U J U

This swirling power inside me

Speaks when there is nothing inside but sores

Void of the healing spirit as the word LOVE

Ever see the glow of the black cat's eyes at night

It is me without pins and dolls

Someone's revenge upon you

Without leaving a trace someone's wounded.


Juju for shadow people trapped in a steel world

Even the fresh blood like me knows

As I move closer to truth

To the other side of my breath

To the earth history of my color awaiting me in the distance.


Yet I hold my course due South like my ancestors

Toward the drum talk   toward the cane and cotton fields

But the veterans say

That we laborers can never own our own souls.

K Kelly McElroy

## Poem for Beginners

deep in the outburst of their misery

the fat gobbling cream puffs to hide their tears

steeped in colors of charcoal

with backstage tales of porcelain

children raising cain

mammies penned to the mat

underneath layers of makeup and clothes

designed for the perfect rape victim


and sit and sit and sit still

with daytime peace work nightmares

charming they feets

and flattening they battle scarred nights


say to  say to never step on anybody's toes

and to keep your behind stuck up in the back

like a black ant

Celebrating 50 • 1968 - 2018
The Legacy of the Muntu Poets of Cleveland

deep in the outburst of their misery

the poor are always in error

their ghosts always out of bounds


as the poor await their debut

while their heads are still warm

dealing with an array of friends from the Big House

for a sniff of slop and a scholarship to charm school


savage this life

episodes of routine trips to the cleaners

from a catalogue of split decisions

hocus-pocus for the Pure-D depraved

yo-yos for the kiddies  trapped in bodies burning up


strange as it seems

fido was born old to learn the necessary tricks

his tambourine tuned up too high

so sick believing that we're living at their expense

so sick believing that slaves can be freed with a song

our folks are in love with dinner music

filled with glee for a pat on the head

for good luck

sorry our beginners have no trumps

milk the coma from our mirage

bring a halt to this eternal honeymoon

accomplished in the backseat joy of our delusions

with no place to call our own

with no title to anything

but our obsession

for bloomers and thrills

hey junebug...some like it hot!

# M.A. Shaheed

## Advancing

Things never changed much for the Dumb Cluck.
Oh, he still had a cold one in the fridge, the TV still
worked. His boss, who he never met wasn't
going to give him a lower mortgage or the 401k back.
He didn't drop the cost of the beer or cigarettes.
No matter how much he did for his boss his situation
was not going to ever change. The stories he loved,
that kept him entertained they wouldn't change either.
He was so dumb that he thought he was doing good for
his folks. The mirrors in his house didn't work either so
he just removed them , like Dracula. Blood is what he
had in common with the count. His boss actually hated
 him and would thank whoever he believed in for the Cluck.
All the time his boss was trying to get away and leave the
Cluck where he found him, because he was not going to take
him with them for sure! When the Cluck got home from a
night of pure hatred he still had cancer, His wife was still
cheating on him, his kids were using heroin.
The doctor bills kept skyrocketing for the 3 dogs. His
neighbor was found to be a serial killer. The guy across
 the street was a school teacher and a pedophile.
He was so screwed up his answer to everything was to
 murder, torture
everybody. He still didn't get a raise. Nothing changed.
Some how he was advancing the cause of humanity.
Well, that's what the TV told him.

# Tabulations

The regrets were lodged in groups.
They were in numbers that were
random. They were arranged from the
things he could remember clearly
and the ones he wanted to forget.

There were the ones that his numbed
conscience would not let him find. The
ones drenched in blood he could
rationalize those. He would compare
them to mosquitoes.

He never regretted his idea that water
was not a right but a privilege. Killing the
poor was his answer to poverty. He was
Pissed off because he couldn't find any one
else in the universe to murder.

At his job he was given a corner office, which
he destroyed within a weeks time. He wanted
to kill his boss because he fired him. He regretted
the fact he couldn't find him. He couldn't imagine
why he got fired! It just didn't add up.

K Kelly McElroy

# The Asterisk

I'm a butcher*, a chef* .I make
candy and candles*

I'm a cop*. I'm a fireman*
I'm a teacher*, a scientist*

I'm an athlete*, a programmer*
a photographer*, a kid*

I'm a reporter*, a cameraman*,
 a criminal*, a clown*. I'm a businessman*

I'm a doctor*, a lawyer*, an Indian chief*
I sell insurance* and cars and trucks*

I'm a soldier* a chemist* **a clergy*** a priest*
I'm a linguist*a genius*.I'm a writer*, a poet*

I 'm etcetera*and etcetera* and etcetera*

I'm an American asterisk* Ask them.

Celebrating 50 • 1968 - 2018
The Legacy of the Muntu Poets of Cleveland

K Kelly McElroy

# Art Nixon

## Highway Markers, Review Mirrors – For Cheryl

Inside the car
In the mirror
The sky has just dissolved a red tablet of sun
And dyed itself    hot pink   maroon
And    now,   black.

Mute and rejected & filed at less than mile intervals
The highway markers sprout in the headlight spray
And wither red in the taillights passing.
The Truth Is:
In the beginning was the end.
Even
The
Orgasm

Begins in a thin wheeze of need,
But soon becomes
A glorious megaphone
Announcing its own
Departure

Even
The
Mystics have sometimes taught there is a death
After life after death...

The shoe presses down and the markers rush up

**Celebrating 50 • 1968 - 2018**
The Legacy of the Muntu Poets of Cleveland

To the windows like obedient phantoms
Where you see them for what they are:
Cheap fixtures to be jettisoned from
The night-long room,
Flash passed and gulped up by the blackness
Leaning full-blown and immovable
All across the car's rear view:
Each beginning existing at the mercy of an ending.

It is what it means
To see chunks
Of highway night-space
After each marker that is passed.
It is what someone said
*They* thought you should have been;
And *more* than you knew yourself to be
It is what it means to have been legally in love.

The highway markers will parade infinity
Across one more state line

Before the night begins to nod,,
It's last cup of strong black coffee
loosened from its fingers

And spills onto the asphalt in an

Obscene libation:

Finally, the night,

Supine in the middle of

The highway: shoeless,

Dirty sock soles on one foot,

K Kelly McElroy

The other barefoot,

Will lay with its mouth gaped bright blue.

From time   to   time    it is
The rearview that is viewed and reviewed
That    mirrors    the    wall of black
You've been speeding through,
With not a trace to betray your direction.
 From    time    to    time until
The Light: the eyes will check.

They *know* there can be
New beginnings    but seem    to    need    more proof,
That you've been
Where you've been

--Art Nixon/1977

# [In Confidence]

Sometimes I awake
In the middle of the night
and I am not there

I have slipped away:
Like a well-used bar of soap in the shower, or
The first dime through a new hole in a worn pocket,
The shadow of a good point--meant to be made--in the heat of debate, or
That fat, yellow balloon-moon tethered to the car for miles, then look again
And it is trapped in a tree, blocked by a billboard, or replaced by a mountain.

I lie there
Fascinated yet overwhelmed
At the terror of being outside myself:
My name and all genetics
Bled out into blackness, deafening silence, immovable and eternal

I brace against its unmentionable depth, and
Sense the length of the unfathomable
that I am in this place

*I inhabit your weight next to me,*
*Listen to the sleeping softness of your breaths*
*And wonder what it's made of:*

*Curiously I touch the dark/gather it*
*In my fingers and brush up against the*
*Awful weight of miracles compressed into*
*This moment,*

*This unexpected Presence*
*This witnessing of God*
*So polite*
*So quiet*
*So discrete...*
*Merely shifting positions*
*In the room*
*When He*
*Thought*
*I was*
*Asleep*
*--Art Nixon 2001*

Celebrating 50 • 1968 - 2018
The Legacy of the Muntu Poets of Cleveland

# Smooth Science

There was a time
When I would
Coax the light back out of the dawn
With my tongue

And gloat over
The infinite
Elixirs I'd brew
With my words

A time when I would stand my ground
Inside my young black skin &
Beg for leg
Like a country boy in bib overalls,
With the Harvest Moon in my voice
And pockets full of
Smooth large stones

So pregnant with myself
I would take a woman's first rejections
As a down payment for my services to be rendered,
A command to lean forward in my science
Explode out the blocks & skim low & quick
Whisking dimes off the tops of hurdles with my ass...

Moons wane.
Petulant waves race after its own impulse/
Eventually receding to low tide/gathered up in the arms of the sea

    Retreating like a woman's desire,
    Kidnapped by her own intuition

Stout trees prop up the skies

And the oak is eventually felled,
It's accountability of time
Irrefutable--right there--in the simple arithmetic
Of its own cross sections

I have traveled the long way around the mountain
To respect the forces that dwell
In the spaces between my words

These days
If I tell you that you are beautiful
You need not take it personally:

I am just the weatherman, baby
Smiling kindly inside the TV box,
Pointing my wand at the map,
And wouldn't dare take the credit
For a sunny day

--Art Nixon/3-31-01

Celebrating 50 • 1968 - 2018
The Legacy of the Muntu Poets of Cleveland

## Yaseen Assami

## A Glass of Lemonade

Oh just a glass of lemonade.
I would snatch the tear drops from your eyes
And rip the love from your heart.
Oh for a glass of lemonade.
I would wade through oceans of blood,
And kill the meaning of desire.
I love you more than sunshine,
But less than moonlight,
And lemonade.
Sometimes I find myself crawling through nightmares
Only to be saved by a glass of lemonade.
Tyme snatches the chill from the refrigerator .
My shadow stands shivering screaming for a glass Of
lemonade,
I set at the table talking to my former tymes.
Watching tomorrow make love to a glass of lemonade.
Wandering through Charlie's mind.
Kicking over trash cans of ideals,burning
Old newspapers.
Terror trembles in the path of death.
Fate hides behind yesterday's excuses,
Watching angry butterflies fling grenades at dead
horses.
While drinking a glass of lemonade

Observing paper progenies play chubby in piles of broken hearts.
Bowls.bells.Birds sing songs of joy
I sit wondering why love wears a mask of lunacy.
Running through a blues song canoodling camels.
Waving goodbye to instanity, Drinking a glass of lemonade.

K Kelly McElroy

## Gorilla Glue DUCT Tape and Spit

Slipping through the cracks,
fate and tyme call on some patient moment before the fifth minute.
looking for some sign of success,clinging to a mustard seed of faith.
Listening to the whispers of deferred dreams,
Dancing on a razors edge,
Looking back at a situation as it clings to the tears of a soul lost in the confusion of a
frustrated affair.
Watching the bitter chill of winter , caress the promise of a warm spring day.
Peering through the heat of summer into a glass of frozen needs of why not.
Dancing with tyme , Looking for your embrace between the flickering lite of the window
pane and the gentle clatter of a broken lantern that reflects the frosty patterns of a cat's
meow.
Holding hands with a forgotten commitment,
ages snatches away the care free uncearinty of youth,
Death stands ever so near uttering the names of past hello's.
Latin rhythms of a flamingo dream reach for the true colors of tomorrows sweat
drenched efforts of slip and tac.

Slowly moving toward the out stretched arms of loneliness,
the voices of despair speak about the gentle ways of truth.
my heart holds the promise of romance,as the gentle breeze of spring,
hums a love you now as never before.

K Kelly McElroy

# Microwave Grits

*Sitting here in the dark surrounded by four corners of a place life has carved from the bitter sweet past of some halfhearted effort to be free from the precautions of a broken man's effort to understand the needs of the many or the nigger next door.*

Listing to the cold winter wind whisper the blues about the coming of spring and tapping a tune about the last storm on a melting snowflake.

Searching for a soft place to land and watching life creep away in the shadows of a forgotten lullaby.

Remembering the song mother sang as she faded away into a place surrounded by hope and desperation

Watching father turn small chances into major provisions as he rehearsed the hopes and dreams of john Coltrane, McKinley Morganfield and Emit Teal.

Waiting for the sun to rise while the roar of a tear etches fond memories of yesterday on tomorrow's goodbye.

Yaseen AsSami

08/25/2013

Celebrating 50 • 1968 - 2018
The Legacy of the Muntu Poets of Cleveland

# Vince Robinson

## STAND

sit
and get caught up in the narratives
interrupted by pleas for cheese
MSGeezus and pizzas
washed down with caffeine
and a Listerine chaser

pharmaceutical solutions bring disease and disaster
followed by words from the pastor
prayers lose the battle with the inevitable

sleepwalking masses OD on data daily
suffering from withdrawal when batteries die

blurry line between the truth and a lie
holds them captive
while history goes untold

secret subversions hidden by diversions
spectacular vernacular disguises meaningless phenomena
as relevant elements of society
sobriety as elusive as world peace

TSA fuels the fire of global mistrust and discontent
from continent to continent

sit
and open your mind to the concept of liberating it

Celebrating 50 • 1968 - 2018
The Legacy of the Muntu Poets of Cleveland

from the grip of control by the Thought Police

mental physicians with negative intentions
in need of intervention by reason
destined to undo centuries of deception
perpetuated with the notion of immaculate conception

melanin virgin earth birthed
cradle of civilization to the corners of the world
leaving footprints and fossils
fluoride-full docile minds filled with trivial finds
succumb to mundanity and vanity
following fast in the footsteps of idols
from titles written in Hollywood glitter by Illuminati
karate on the brain designed to make you

sit
and do nothing as your slavery fades into eternity
failing to see the writing in the sky
chemtrails in them tales they tell to pacify
confuse and defy
culls nimbus cirrus symmetry in azure

hospital bill
hundred dollar pill
oxycontin methadone thrill
heroin deaths fill Capitol hill
suicidal psychos kill at will

sit
and be still

stand
and be free

K Kelly McElroy

## B Real

# America, Girl You Slippin'

AMERIKA, AMERIKA GOD SHED HIS LIGHT ON THEE...

Amerika one hell of of a place

but you ask GOD shed upon you

THEE Heavenly grace

you kill people you steal people

other countries you lay to waste

you come from evil you breed evil

YOU ARE EVIL!!

the time has come again for you to

LET MY PEOPLE GO

free the peoples minds

from your lies and wicked fairy tales

tell the truth about your roots

so i can overstand why it is i do what i do

## Celebrating 50 • 1968 - 2018
### The Legacy of the Muntu Poets of Cleveland

i am a product of your enviroment

your CULT-TURE

you are the reason i chase my sisters

your material trinkets like a vulture

is how and american lives

love waxed cold

hate created over the years

taught to love the lies and hate the truth

taught to hate and depsise me

and i look just like you

taught to put on a mask a disguise

dont let your real feelins show through

amerika was built on lies

and thats all babylon will ever produce


Amerika girl you slippin

responsible for the lives of many

you got the people stuck

trying to get the latest gigets and gadgets

K Kelly McElroy

your programing marinating the minds

of yours his hers and my kind

you dont obey the ways and customs

of THEE true GOD in the Heavens above

you teach more hate to the children

and show less love

took thy lord out of schools

and replaced THEE with blood

now your the chicken head hoodrat

scurvy punk tramp knuckle head rich broad

enter-tainting the minds with

your tell/lie/vision shows

brothers and sisters going at each others throats

on the tv courts

people putting thier bussiness in the streets

on the jerry springer show

i mean how you gone bring me on national

tell/lie/vision

and tell me this women is a man i been kissin

im bout to catch a case wait.....

no i aint cause i wouldnt even show up. anyway

remeber the murders at the Collinbine school episode

well how many copycats you think would have followed

if that story was never told

get right girl you slippin

naked on the beach

plegde ligions to a star spangled banner

is what you preach

what about the convenents we made

family friends my peeps in the streets

i dont care what religion you practice or teach

the covenents pertain to each and every one of us

and our LORD thy GOD is watching every little thing

WE DO

so my people to yourself you got to be true

peace one love from b-real to you

# Girl I Wanna Vibe

Girl i wanna vibe off your vibe and you vibe off mine

our anything and everything for ever enter-twined

if im across the ocean sailling down the nile river

my third eye connects with yours and i say come hither

come hither my sweet

thee carob queen of my dreams

ill be your Adam and you can be my Eve

ill be the mind guide we live and you

the protecter of our inner organs our soulsmy heart my rib

i close my seeing eyes contemplate meditate and visualize

you do the same

as we ride the spirit across the plains

they connect come together

our minds our bodies our souls embrace

i open my eyes and see your lovly lovly face

darkbrown mahogany complexion

matching the windows of your soul

i see your full lips yeah girl

you got the kind of beauty that will make a weak man slip

## Celebrating 50 • 1968 - 2018
### The Legacy of the Muntu Poets of Cleveland

but im strong and you know this if not better get hip

see i aint for them games i leave that for them lames

but anyway back to the vibe you and i on the plains

gliding high descovering the UNI-VERSE

as we rise no need to rush we take our time

circling clouds dodging rainstorms

absorbing feelings never ever felt before

theres a cosmic serge of energy flowing through our heavens

we say a prayer for the sabbaht has just begun

praise the SPIRIT of YAH as we journey up above

soaring never ending heights our Yah minds intact

hey queeen you feelin me picture that

now the season for the planting of our seed is upon us

but just like our THEE CREATOR in the Image of THEE are we

so we say be and what it is shall be

a hardy harvest a boy a girl

tummies full of love nurishment and joy

a never ending cycle of life everlasting

no more pain no more sorrow

loving memories of yesterdays and i cant wait until tomorrows

## Danielle Dixon

# Ain't Dat Some Shit

What If...
    Your parents didn't fail you?
What if...
    Their assignment with you
    Was to keep you alive until you could keep yourself?
    And look at you now
    Livin' and shit!

    Ain't dat some shit?
    Ain't DAT some shit?
What if...
    They were just mere mortals with issues?
What if...
    They learned more from you
    Than you ever could from them?
What if...
    Your strength
    Turns out to be their salvation?

    Ain't dat some shit?
    Ain't DAT some shit?
What if...
    That narrative you tell the world
    'bout how "It's just Me, Myself, and I"
    That you say is your mantra
    Because it steel's your nerves
    So you don't get disappointed by a world
        That doesn't love you
    Actually, creates the reality
    That the world doesn't love you?

# Celebrating 50 • 1968 - 2018
## The Legacy of the Muntu Poets of Cleveland

What if...
    Love never came to stay
    Because You
        Never set a place for it at your table?
    But you shacked up
    With that crush    you swore you couldn't breathe without
    Whose presence choked the life out of you.

    Ain't dat some shit?
    Ain't DAT some shit?
What if...
    You had help the whole time
    But never asked for it?
What if...
    The guardian angel
    That wants so badly to help you succeed
    Sits bound, gagged and forgotten
    By YOUR negativity and lack of action?

    Ain't dat some shit?
    Ain't DAT some shit?
What if...
    Our reality
    Is someone else's short sighted version
    Of a fantasy?
    And...
What if...
    The unrealistic things we fantasize about
    Are the things we really are capable of?
What if...
    Normalcy
    Was really abnormal
    And dysfunction
    Is the first sign you're alive?
What if...
    Conformity

      Creates chaos?
What if...
      You never struggled?
What if...
      You never felt the urgency
      Of needing to achieve your goal the first time
      Because there's an ass whoopin'
      Waiting for your failure?
What if...
      You never learned the lessons
      You got from the struggle
      That forged you into the warrior you are today?
What if...
      The lesson is in the process
      And not the result?

      Ain't dat some shit?
      Ain't DAT some shit?

                                       Danielle N Dixon
                                       10/28/2016

# Beware

Beware of the slave

That don't wanna be free

They'll sell you out

If you try to flee

Their only goal for crowning grace

Is just to take the master's place.


Danielle N Dixon 7-15-2016

K Kelly McElroy

# I Am Fabulous

I. Am. Fabulous!

I was fabulous 20 years ago
I'll be fabulous 20 years from now
When I'm dead
    I'll be dead and fabulous
I'll be fabulous at 500lbs or 99lbs soaking wet
I'm fabulous when I'm pretty
Being ugly doesn't stop me from being fabulous
I am fabulous in abundance
When I lack resources
    I'm resourcefully fabulous
I was born fabulous
    With the ability to generate fabulousness
My fabulous is a self- contained unit
It morphs, changes, and reinvents itself
    As it sees fit
My fabulous does not need your approval
Yet it remains open to be inspired
    By other people's fabulousness
Because the world needs fabulous people
Playing meek never inspired anyone
And when I see how you wear fabulousness
    Whether you strut it
    Sashay it
    Limp it
    Crutch it
    Or roll it in a wheelchair
I will always applaud it
Because one person's fabulousness does not diminish another's
Fabulousness is infinite
And the world needs your rendition

Celebrating 50 • 1968 - 2018
The Legacy of the Muntu Poets of Cleveland

    Of unapologetic fabulousness
    To be represented
    Right Here
    Right now
    Right where you stand

Danielle Dixon 8/5/2016

K Kelly McElroy

## VitaGold

# Am I the Reason

Am I the reason that your heart breaks like a shattered mirror? Pieces thrown against time unretrievable.
Am I the reason that silent tears leave streaks in the quite of night leaving behind unseen scars?
Am I the reason that bitterness has taken over a once loving heart that now beats with the rhythm of scorn?
Am I the reason that your smile has faded into black no longer carrying the shine that I once fell in love with?
Am I the reason that my own heart bleeds for love I can't seem to keep no matter how hard I seek?
Am I the reason that the thing I want the most continues to slip through my fingers even when I think I have a strong grip?
I just need to know... am I the reason?

# Iron Sharpens Iron

Like minds give to same thoughts creating a mist of fulfilling experience.
Writers block broken when iron sharpens iron creativity sparks a fire.
Ink begins to flow mind goes on overload with words lost in purgatory.
My paper sings a song happy that I've finally come home to awaken a spirit that was lost.
It all comes so easy forgot what this release could be almost better than an orgasm.
Words flow slow and easy like two lovers creating life.
My strife escapes me with each letter that releases a comfort that is a soothing salve to my soul.
Oh these words how I have missed you and the healing that you bring.
I am open to your power and embrace this moment like a Christian getting baptized. Anointed with a gift all I needed was the right push to reignite a fire deep in my being.
I am reawakened alive with purpose to give these words a new life to share with anyone that hears.
I am truly alive with poetry.

# K Kelly

## I Know...

Sometimes life can be so unsure
I wonder as I look at the night shy
Sometimes – I'm scared and insecure
Why? – I really wonder why

I remember when I felt on top of the world
It did not seem – that feeling would end
Reality – is sometimes very sobering
I wonder – if I could handle it again

Sometimes, I really... I really don't know

I don't know – what the next hour brings
Don't know – the length of my days
Don't know – if the next time I'll feel real love
Don't know – my creator's ways

I wish – I could peer into the future
Wish – I could tell you for sure
Wish – that all your dreams come true
Wish – that I could make you feel secure

But I know... I really do know

That good things come to those with pure hearts

**Celebrating 50 • 1968 - 2018**
**The Legacy of the Muntu Poets of Cleveland**

That spirit lives an eternity
That you can defeat all your fears
That true happiness – can be a reality

One day – it's going to be real
One day – it's going to be like it should
One day – it's going to be so beautiful
One day – it's going to feel so good

Yes, I know... I really do know

I really know – that real love endures
Really know – when someone's sincere
Really know – I'm going to try
Really know – that God really cares

There are some things that can't be disputed
Yes – some thigs are for sure
No – it's not conditional
What – my feelings are pure

Yes, I know... So what are you going to do?

I know – it's real scary sometimes
Know – you been lied to before
Know - you deserve the very best
Know – you want to have more

Do you know? Do you really, really know?

Do you know – sometimes I'm really scared

Do you know – my heart is really pure
Do you know – real love reigns supreme
Do you know – there's no choice but to endure

Do you know – sometimes dreams do come true
Do you know – there's a hand to catch, when you fall
Do you know – spirit lives an eternity
Do you know – someone hears your call…

I know… I really do know

Celebrating 50 • 1968 - 2018
The Legacy of the Muntu Poets of Cleveland

# Star Child

Like the sunlight brilliant, moon and stars
An airy breeze and cavernous space
True beauty is unique and that you are
I see eternal light when I see your face

What's so funny is that I just met you today
Deep caramel, chocolaty fine
Normally I would be scared - but I'm OK
Silly me, I wonder if you could be mine

So savoir faire, makes old men stare
More than just a gorgeous physical form
I know I don't really know you – yet, I care
The reason must be, you're beyond the norm

Your vibration gives me chills
For some reason, I don't have to ask why
Just met you – but being away from you make me ill
Gotta get myself together, yet can't pass her by

Mesmerized when she looks me in the eye
My heart misses a beat, the way she makes me feel
I'm usually outgoing, but for some reason I feel shy
It's not infatuation – this feeling is real

Could it be love? Because it's not about me
Her presence is near, yet I'm in the stars
Can I contain her essence? I guess I'll see
She's a thousand light years away – yet never far

As I land back on earth, back into the atmosphere

K Kelly McElroy

My thoughts, sensations, and spirit recompress
Serenity, peace and love emit, with no fear
I realize if I want her I must be truly sincere – no finesse (well, maybe just a little)


Can you hear my thoughts? I'm sure you do
The experience has been shocking, yet soulfully mild
Regardless of what happens, I truly want the best for you
You, that shiny, that brilliant, that beautiful, that lovely – Star Child

# True Love

The word LOVE, so overused and abused
Like the word JAZZ
We don't know where to put non-improvised instrumentals
We're so confused

Truth is, real love is really true
Love is true in the beginning
The end and in between
Everything is everything, and love reigns supreme

This may be true
But – what does it really mean?

Truth is, love is really true
Love is the source of everything in existence
From embryonic creation
To all the wonderful palettes and colors of life

Despite any opposition, it remains persistent
This is true because, love is really true

Love sometimes escapes definition
Yet, a mere child knows in in their heart
Love seeks harmony in its improvisation

Love expresses itself from the spirit and soul
From which it could never part
It's true, because it is
Truly, it's so

Even though true love is truly perfect
It's not always perfectly expressed
Love is the admission of being wrong at times

K Kelly McElroy

And throwing pride to the side


It always strives for musical harmony
And always tries its best
For true love is the truth
And wonderfully true it is

It forgives, yet not forgets
For love is not blind
It forgives because negativity and love cannot coexist
It can be done with love because it always strives to be kind

Loving truly, is true love indeed – not just words
If amorous expressions go unrequited
Love still remains, even at a distance
It strives to understand others, and never is spited

True love is truly strong indeed, Truly it is
If hatred, envy, strife or any other negative energy come its way
Love strives for wonder endings, even if dissonant notes are played
Love's dedication to beauty holds sway

Love is simply love
Yes, it is true
Love is far more than just words or even thoughts
It's what we are

Love can't be selfish
An must look out for the needs of others
Love really is so brilliant and shines brighter than any star

Love is, really love is – it's true
Love can never hate another
Because it understands that all creation is one

Love is eternal, love is real
True love really is true
Because the act of showing true love is never done

As time eternal proceeds
Man certainly must look and pray above
Symphonies of prayers, wishes, wonderment, and questions arise
What would the world be like
If everyone really had – True love…

# About the Author

At the helm of Uptown Media Joint Ventures, K Kelly is following his passion of helping authors get their viable stories published and marketed to their readers! This passion includes expanding the audiences for recording artists and freelance journalists, as well!

K Kelly is an avid Modern Jazz enthusiast. He proudly owns a vintage collection of over 1000 classic jazz CDs. His first jazz book, a buying guide, *Best of the Best Modern Jazz* was an effort to compile his significant knowledge of the genre to assist others who want to develop and enjoy their own modern jazz collection. Modern jazz Classics expands on the concept by adding biographical information for key musicians of the modern jazz era.

K Kelly is the author of the book, *Modern Jazz Classics.* He is a contributor to Original Muntu Poet Robert Fleming's noted work *Free Jazz* and, a concise, yet comprehensive, book on the best of modern jazz albums.

K Kelly would like to give thanks all the Original Muntu Poets who have been indispensable in the development of Uptown Media, with special thanks to Russell Atkins, M.A. Shaheed. Art Nixon, Robert Fleming, and Yaseen Assami.

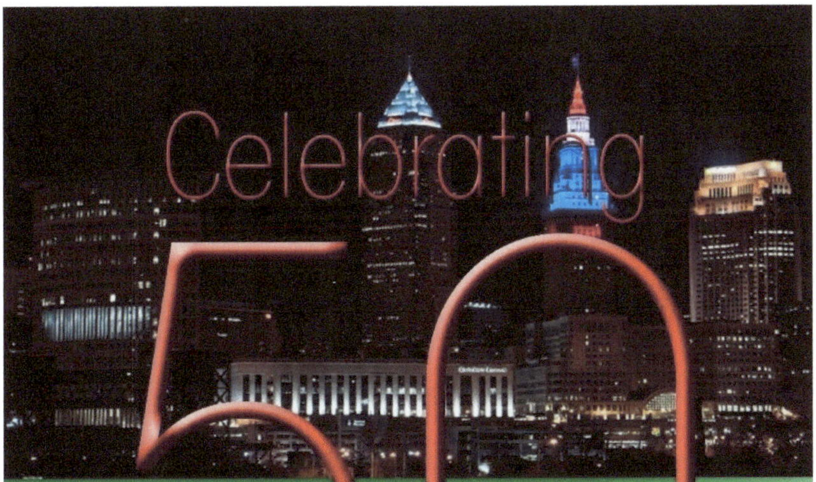

# Celebrating 50

## The Legacy of the Muntu Poets of Cleveland

### 1968 – 2018

www.ingramcontent.com/pod-product-compliance
Lightning Source LLC
Chambersburg PA
CBHW041959150426
43194CB00002B/66